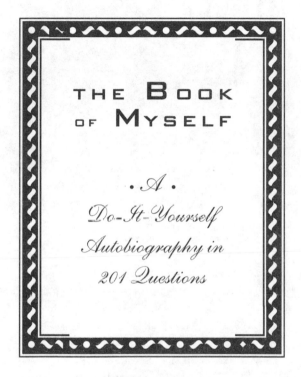

THE BOOK OF MYSELF

· A ·

Do-It-Yourself
Autobiography in
201 Questions

CARL & DAVID MARSHALL

HYPERION
New York

Library of Congress Cataloging-in-Publication Data

Marshall, Carl, b. 1903
The book of myself : a do-it-yourself autobiography in 201
questions / Carl & David Marshall. — 1st ed.
p. cm.
ISBN 0-7868-6250-5
1. Autobiography. 2. Diaries. I Marshall, David, 1956– II. Title.
CT25.M27 1997
808'.06692—dc20
96-36072 CIP

Designed by Claudyne Bianco Bedell

First Edition
17   19   20   18   16

To Our Children:

GENE AND KARLDENE, EMILY AND BENJAMIN

As your teachers we have become humble students

Contents

Early Years

Middle Years

Later Years

How to Write Your Own Autobiography

How?

- Here are 201 prompts to help you begin telling your special story. You fill in the rest.

- Three main sections, or chronological life phases, cover the early, middle, and later years. It is up to you to decide where one section leaves off and the next begins for your own life.

- Each phase of life is broken down into five subjects covering experiences about family, friends, education, work, and the world. These subjects are located at the bottom of the page.

- The table of contents will help you find a certain life phase and subject quickly. Start anywhere you want.

Who? and When?

- IF YOU ARE 91 YEARS OLD, LIKE ONE OF THE CO-AUTHORS, YOU ARE IN A POSITION TO WRITE DOWN ALMOST THE WHOLE STORY. GET HELP FROM YOUR LOVED ONES TO REMEMBER SPECIAL MOMENTS.

- IF YOU ARE ONE OR TWO GENERATIONS YOUNGER YOU CAN STILL START THE STORY, SINCE AT LEAST YOUR EARLY YEARS ARE NOW BEHIND YOU AND THE MEMORIES ARE STILL FRESH IN YOUR MIND. OR GIVE THIS BOOK TO A LOVED ONE TO FILL OUT AND RETURN TO YOU.

- IF YOU ARE STILL IN YOUR EARLY YEARS YOU CAN START THE STORY AND FILL IT OUT AS YOU GO. BY SEARCHING AHEAD FOR EXPERIENCES YET TO COME YOU MAY RECOGNIZE THEM AS THEY APPEAR. OR GIVE THE BOOK TO A LOVED ONE TO FILL OUT AND RETURN TO YOU.

What Do I Do With This Book After It Is Filled Out?

- GIVE IT TO YOUR CHILDREN OR GRANDCHILDREN.

- GIVE IT TO A SPECIAL FRIEND.

- KEEP IT WITH YOUR FAMILY HEIRLOOMS.

- This may just be the beginning. Perhaps you may want to write down additional stories in a similar fashion and put them in the book.

- You do not have to fill out all the questions. Fill in only what you want. It is complete when you say it is.

- Read it cover to cover; reflect and rejoice in the wonder of life's experiences.

Introduction

I WAS BORN IN 1903 AND HAVE JUST CELEBRATED MY
91ST BIRTHDAY WITH GLADYS, MY WIFE OF 68 YEARS.
WE HAVE A SON AND DAUGHTER, EIGHT WONDERFUL
GRANDCHILDREN, AND SO MANY GREAT-GRANDCHILDREN
I CANNOT KEEP TRACK OF THEM ALL. TWO YEARS AGO MY
DAUGHTER KARLDENE HELPED ME WRITE MY MEMOIRS. IT
WAS AN EXHILARATING EXPERIENCE TO TELL THE STORIES
OF MY CHILDHOOD, YOUNG ADULTHOOD, AND LATER
YEARS IN A WAY THAT COULD BE PASSED ON TO FUTURE
GENERATIONS. MY FAMILY LOVED IT. MY FRIENDS WERE
ENVIOUS, BUT MOST OF THEM FELT IT WOULD BE TOO DIF-
FICULT FOR THEM TO DO THE SAME. AFTER ALL, IT TOOK
ME OVER A YEAR TO WRITE WITH MY DAUGHTER DOING ALL
THE TYPING AND ASSEMBLING.

SO WHEN MY GRANDSON DAVID APPROACHED ME
WITH A PLAN FOR A SIMPLE BOOK THAT WOULD HELP PEO-
PLE BEGIN TELLING THEIR STORIES, I JUMPED AT THE
CHANCE TO CO-WRITE IT. WHAT WE HAVE DONE HERE IS
GIVE YOU THE SKELETON TO YOUR STORY. YOU PROVIDE
THE MEAT ON THE BONES. AFTER ALL, EVERYONE HAS
STORIES TO TELL ABOUT FAMILY, FRIENDS, EDUCATION,
WORK, AND THE WORLD DURING THE DIFFERENT PHASES
OF LIFE.

I AM NEARING THE END OF MY JOURNEY NOW. BUT
BEFORE I GO I WANTED MY FAMILY AND LOVED ONES TO
KNOW MY STORIES, BIG OR SMALL, DEEP OR SHALLOW,
KNOWN OR UNKNOWN. I HAVE LEARNED A LOT DURING
THESE LAST NINE DECADES AND WANT TO SHARE THIS

WITH THE NEXT THREE GENERATIONS. I KNOW YOU DO TOO.
BEFORE YOU GO, LET THEM KNOW.

    CARL E. MARSHALL

(GRANDPA CARL PASSED AWAY PRIOR TO THE PUBLICA-
TION OF THIS BOOK.)

I GREW UP IN THE 60S AND 70S AND WILL SOON BE
CELEBRATING MY 39TH BIRTHDAY WITH KATE, MY WIFE OF
TEN YEARS. WE HAVE TWO YOUNG CHILDREN AND LOOK FOR-
WARD TO MANY OF OUR BEST YEARS STILL AHEAD OF US.
WE ARE WATCHING OUR PARENTS AND GRANDPARENTS
GROW OLDER NOW WITH TREPIDATION AND AWE;
TREPIDATION IN REALIZING THAT THEY WILL NOT BE WITH US
FOREVER AND AWE IN REALIZING THE WISDOM ABOUT LIFE
THEY CARRY WITH THEM. GRANDPA CARL TAUGHT ME TO
REACH FOR THE STARS AND TO BELIEVE IN MYSELF EVEN IF
OTHERS LOSE THEIR FAITH. HE ALSO WORKED ME HARD BUT
I HAVE TO ADMIT, SUCH TASKS AS BRICKLAYING IN HIS
BACKYARD HELPED STRENGTHEN MY WORK ETHIC. AND HE
SHOWED ME HOW TO TREAT MATH AS AN ADVENTURE
INSTEAD OF A CHORE.

I HAVE ALWAYS LOVED HEARING GRANDPA SPIN YARNS
AROUND THE DINNER TABLE. THEY HELPED ME TO KNOW HIM
MORE INTIMATELY. I WANTED TO FIND A WAY TO ASK HIM
ABOUT ALL THE DIFFERENT AREAS OF HIS LIFE AND TO SAVE
WHAT HE TOLD ME, EVEN SOME OF THE LITTLE TIDBITS THAT
HE WOULD NEVER THINK TO ADD HIMSELF. IT NOW COM-
FORTS ME TO KNOW THAT LONG AFTER GRANDPA CARL IS
GONE I WILL STILL HAVE THIS LITTLE BOOK OF TREASURES
TO SHARE WITH MY CHILDREN AND GRANDCHILDREN. I HOPE

THIS COLLECTION OF LIFE STORIES WILL HELP YOU TO ALSO
BEGIN SHARING YOUR STORIES WITH THOSE WHO WILL CARRY
ON IN YOUR PATH.

David P. Marshall

EARLY YEARS

ONE OF MOM'S TRAITS I ADMIRED WAS:

It really took me a while to think on this one. But then I realized something about my mother. She hasn't ever been the Greatest (or the Worst) what she has always been is someone who "tried". Maybe not as hard as others, but she was at least, and still is TRYING. Seems to be how she makes her way into the world and thru her days. She wakes up and tries. I never have thought much on her successes or her failures, but I know she tried it as it came to her. That is a good thing. I like to think she makes it more than she failed.

FAMILY 3

If I HAD ANY TROUBLE WITH MOM GROWING UP, IT WAS IN THIS AREA:

ONE OF DAD'S TRAITS I ADMIRED WAS:

*I*F, GROWING UP, I HAD ANY TROUBLE WITH DAD, IT WAS IN THIS AREA:

I REMEMBER GETTING INTO TROUBLE WITH MY
PARENTS ON THIS OCCASION:

THIS IS HOW WE USUALLY ATE DINNER AS A FAMILY:

A HABIT I PICKED UP DURING MY EARLY YEARS WAS:

*M*y PARENTS FELT STRONGLY ABOUT PASSING
ON THESE LESSONS:

THIS PERSON IN MY FAMILY WAS MORE SERIOUS THAN THE REST:

*T*HIS PERSON IN MY FAMILY WAS FUNNIER THAN THE REST:

_T_HIS PRESENT I GOT FROM MY PARENTS REALLY
STICKS IN MY MEMORY:

WHAT I REMEMBER ABOUT MY FIRST TRIP(S) TO THE HOSPITAL:

ONE OF MY MOST MEMORABLE TOYS WAS:

$\mathcal{T}$HIS IS HOW MY FAMILY CELEBRATED CHRISTMAS OR CHANUKAH:

THIS IS WHAT WE USUALLY DID AT THANKSGIVING:

$\mathcal{I}$ WANT YOU TO KNOW THIS ABOUT MY
GRANDMOTHER(S):

I WANT YOU TO KNOW THIS ABOUT MY GRANDFATHER(S):

*I*F I REMEMBER ANYTHING ABOUT MY GREAT-GRANDPARENTS IT IS THIS:

*T*HE COUNTRY OR COUNTRIES MY ANCESTORS
CAME FROM WAS:

$\mathcal{M}$Y HAIRSTYLE(S) AND NATURAL HAIR COLOR GROWING UP WERE:

$\mathcal{M}$Y FAMILY'S FIRST TV/COMPUTER WAS IN
THE YEAR:...ONE OF MY FAVORITE TV OR SOFTWARE

PROGRAMS WAS:

FAMILY   23

$\mathcal{I}$N THE AFTERNOONS AFTER SCHOOL I USED TO:

Games I liked to play as a child and youth were:

WHAT I LIKED ABOUT MY SIBLINGS WAS:

$\mathcal{P}$EOPLE DESCRIBED ME AS A CHILD IN THIS WAY:

WE HAD THESE PETS OR ACCESS TO OTHER ANIMALS GROWING UP:

THIS PERSON SIGNIFICANTLY INFLUENCED MY LIFE GROWING UP:

$\mathcal{M}$Y BEST FRIEND DURING CHILDHOOD WAS:

I ADMIRED THIS FRIEND BECAUSE OF THE
FOLLOWING TALENTS:

I WAS GENERALLY POPULAR OR UNPOPULAR
BECAUSE:

$\mathcal{I}$ HELPED A FRIEND GREATLY ON THIS OCCASION:

THIS WAS A PARTICULARLY DANGEROUS THING I DID WITH A FRIEND:

$\mathcal{I}$ REMEMBER WELL THIS BIRTHDAY PARTY I HAD
WITH MY FRIENDS:

I WANTED THIS PERSON TO BE MY FRIEND BUT
THE FEELING WAS NOT MUTUAL:

$\mathcal{I}$ HAD A CHILDHOOD CRUSH ON THIS PERSON:

A MEMORABLE ADOLESCENT SWEETHEART WAS:

WHAT MY FRIENDS AND I LIKED BEST TO DO TOGETHER WAS:

*I*F MY PARENTS HAD ONLY KNOWN! I DID THIS
FORBIDDEN THING WITH MY FRIENDS:

I REALLY ENJOYED THIS GRADE IN ELEMENTARY
SCHOOL:

ONE OF MY MOST MEMORABLE TEACHERS IN ELEMENTARY SCHOOL WAS:

$\mathscr{I}$ HAD A LOT OF FUN WITH THIS SUBJECT IN
ELEMENTARY SCHOOL:

I HAD SOME TROUBLE WITH THIS SUBJECT IN JUNIOR HIGH OR HIGH SCHOOL:

$\mathscr{I}$ REALLY ENJOYED THIS JUNIOR HIGH OR HIGH SCHOOL GRADE:

ONE OF MY MOST MEMORABLE TEACHERS IN
JUNIOR HIGH OR HIGH SCHOOL WAS:

I LIKED THIS SUBJECT A LOT IN JUNIOR HIGH OR
HIGH SCHOOL:

WHEN I WAS VERY YOUNG I THOUGHT I WOULD BE THIS WHEN I GREW UP:

*I*F I DIDN'T GRADUATE FROM HIGH SCHOOL IT WAS
BECAUSE:

THIS IS WHY I DID OR DID NOT GO TO COLLEGE:

*I*F I ATTENDED COLLEGE ONE OF MY STRONGEST
MEMORIES WAS:

*T*HIS IS ONE OF THE MOST IMPORTANT THINGS
ABOUT LIFE I LEARNED IN SCHOOL:

*T*HIS IS HOW I GOT TO SCHOOL EACH MORNING IN MY EARLY YEARS:

ONE OF MY EARLIEST MEMORIES ABOUT SCHOOL
WAS:

*T*HESE WERE MY FAVORITE SPORTS IN SCHOOL:

ONE OF MY FAVORITE KINDS OF HOMEWORK WAS:

_M_Y ELEMENTARY AND HIGH SCHOOLS COULD BE DESCRIBED AS: (SMALL/LARGE, PUBLIC/PRIVATE, ACADEMIC/VOCATIONAL...)

_M_ Y TEACHERS GENERALLY DESCRIBED ME AS
THIS KIND OF STUDENT:

$\mathcal{M}$Y RELIGIOUS TRAINING GROWING UP WAS:

$\mathcal{M}$Y FAVORITE MENTOR-ROLE MODEL IN
COLLEGE OR TRADE SCHOOL WAS:

WHAT I ENJOYED DOING MOST AFTER SCHOOL WAS:

I REMEMBER THESE CHORES GROWING UP:

$\mathcal{M}$Y FIRST JOB FOR PAY WAS:

I ENJOYED THIS PARTICULAR WORK ASSIGNMENT:

I TOOK CARE OF THIS PERSON OR PERSONS GROWING UP:

I REMEMBER THIS ABOUT MY MOTHER'S WORK AND RESPONSIBILITIES:

I REMEMBER THIS ABOUT MY FATHER'S WORK AND RESPONSIBILITIES:

I HATED THIS PARTICULAR WORK ASSIGNMENT:

$\mathcal{T}$HIS IS THE PROFESSION THAT I OFTEN
MENTIONED WHEN PEOPLE ASKED ME WHAT I WAS
GOING TO BE WHEN I GREW UP:

I DISLIKED THIS RESPONSIBILITY/WORK GROWING UP BUT IT HAS PROVED TO BE VERY HELPFUL TO ME AS AN ADULT:

*M*Y MEMORIES OF THE BIGGEST WAR OR
SERIOUS CONFLICT DURING MY EARLY YEARS ARE
THESE:

THIS IS WHAT WAR MEANT TO ME GROWING UP:

$\mathcal{T}$HIS WAS A BIG WARTIME EVENT THAT MARKED A TURNING POINT IN THE WORLD (E.G. D-DAY OR EVACUATION OF SAIGON):

I LIKED THIS KIND OF MUSIC AND THESE MUSICIANS GROWING UP:

THE CLOTHES FASHIONS OF MY CHILDHOOD WERE:

_S_OME OF MY FAVORITE HOLLYWOOD ACTORS AND ACTRESSES WERE: ...I LIKED THESE QUALITIES ABOUT THEM:

I REMEMBER WHEN THESE TECHNOLOGICAL ADVANCES WERE MADE:

*M*Y PARENTS FELT THIS WAY ABOUT POLITICS:

"My WORLD" CONSISTED OF THIS GEOGRAPHICAL AREA:

MIDDLE YEARS

*F*OR A WHILE I THOUGHT I WOULD MARRY THIS
PERSON, BUT I DIDN'T:

My FIRST SERIOUS ROMANCE WAS WITH:

I REGRETTABLY LOST TOUCH WITH THIS FAMILY MEMBER AFTER WE GREW UP:

I KEPT THIS SECRET FROM ALMOST EVERYONE:

ONE OF MY MOM'S STRONGEST CHARACTERISTICS WAS:

ONE OF MY DAD'S STRONGEST TRAITS WAS:

_T_HIS ISSUE CAUSED A GREAT RIFT BETWEEN ME
AND MY PARENTS:

WE RECONCILED AFTER THIS HAPPENED:

*M*Y HAIRSTYLE(S) AND HAIR COLOR DURING THESE YEARS WAS:

THE STORY ABOUT HOW I BECAME ENGAGED IS:

$\mathcal{I}$ REMEMBER MY WEDDING WELL:

THIS IS HOW WE DECIDED HOW MANY CHILDREN TO HAVE:

I REMEMBER THE BIRTH(S) OF OUR CHILD(REN) WELL:

I REMEMBER THESE FUNNY INCIDENTS ABOUT
THE CHILDREN WHEN THEY WERE YOUNG:

SOME OF THE THINGS I LOVED DOING WITH MY FAMILY WERE:

*T*HIS WAS A PARTICULARLY MEMORABLE VACATION WITH MY LOVED ONES:

*T*HIS WAS A TIME I GOT VERY ANGRY WITH MY
CHILDREN:

*T*HIS HEALTH PROBLEM WAS VERY SCARY FOR MY FAMILY:

THIS WAS A SERIOUS ACCIDENT I REMEMBER:

$\mathcal{W}$E HAD THESE PETS:

$\mathcal{M}$Y PARENTS PLAYED THIS KIND OF GRANDPARENT ROLE TO MY CHILDREN:

THIS IS THE PART OF MY PARENTING I AM PARTICULARLY PROUD OF:

$\mathcal{T}$HIS IS THE PART OF MY PARENTING WHERE I THINK I COULD HAVE DONE BETTER:

*T*HIS WAS A LONELY BIRTHDAY FOR ME WITHOUT MY FAMILY:

*M*Y BROTHER(S), AND/OR SISTER(S) AND I ACTED THIS WAY TOWARD EACH OTHER:

$\mathcal{M}$Y BEST FRIEND AFTER I LEFT HOME WAS:

*T*HESE PEOPLE WERE MY BEST FRIENDS IN MY
MIDDLE YEARS:

TRUE FRIENDSHIP TO ME MEANS:

THIS PERSON HELPED TO SAVE MY LIFE:

$\mathcal{I}$ REMEMBER THIS EMBARRASSING INCIDENT WITH
A GOOD FRIEND:

*O*NE OF THE WAYS I LIKED TO ENTERTAIN
FRIENDS/GUESTS WAS:

WHEN I THINK OF COMPASSION AND
GOODNESS I THINK OF THIS PERSON:

ONE BIG MISUNDERSTANDING I HAD WITH A FRIEND WAS:

I LEARNED TO TAKE MYSELF LESS SERIOUSLY THROUGH MY FRIENDSHIP WITH:

I HAVE ALWAYS FELT THAT THIS PERSON
BETRAYED ME EVEN THOUGH I WAS ALWAYS LOYAL TO
HIM/HER:

THIS IS THE SPORT I MOST ENJOYED WATCHING OR ATTENDING WITH FRIENDS:

THE ACTIVITY THAT I AND MY FRIENDS MOST OFTEN ENGAGED IN WAS:

A VERY DIFFICULT EDUCATIONAL EXPERIENCE FOR ME WAS:

*T*HESE ARE THE KINDS OF BOOKS I ENJOY
READING MOST:

ONE BOOK THAT HAD A VERY STRONG IMPACT ON ME WAS:

ONE OF MY FAVORITE MAGAZINES IN MY MIDDLE
YEARS WAS:

The subject(s) I always wanted to learn more about as an adult but never did was:

A YEAR IN WHICH I LEARNED A LOT OF NEW SKILLS WAS:

A SEMINAR OR WORKSHOP WHICH REALLY STUCK WITH ME:

THE WAY I LIKED BEST TO LEARN WAS:

$\mathcal{M}$ Y INVOLVEMENT IN RELIGION AS AN ADULT WAS:

THIS IS AN AREA I WAS ABLE TO TEACH WELL TO
OTHERS:

ONE THING I REGRET THAT I NEVER GOT TO EXPLORE:

ONE OF MY ACCOMPLISHMENTS I AM MOST PROUD OF IS:

THIS PERSON WAS A MENTOR FOR ME WHO REALLY HELPED ME IN MY CAREER:

*T*HIS WAS ONE OF THE MOST DIFFICULT BOSSES I HAD TO CONTEND WITH:

I REALLY LIKED WORKING WITH THIS PERSON:

$\mathcal{M}$Y MILITARY EXPERIENCE AS AN ADULT WAS:

Things I Liked About My Work Included:

$\mathcal{I}$F I COULD HAVE CHANGED PROFESSIONS IN MID-STREAM I WOULD HAVE BECOME A:

I STRIVED TO BE THIS KIND OF WORKER WITH THESE QUALITIES:

*S*OME HOUSEHOLD CHORES I ENJOYED AND SOME
I DIDN'T INCLUDE:

*I*F I COULD HAVE CHANGED THE BALANCE
BETWEEN WORK, FAMILY, AND PLAY I WOULD HAVE
DONE SO IN THIS WAY:

THE VALUES I ADHERED TO AS AN ADULT WERE:

$\mathcal{M}$Y FAVORITE HOBBY AT THE TIME WAS:

I REGRET HAVING BURNED THIS BRIDGE:

$\mathcal{I}$ WORKED FOR THESE COMPANIES OR
INSTITUTIONS PRIOR TO RETIREMENT:

THINGS I DISLIKED ABOUT MY WORK INCLUDED:

THESE ARE THE PRESIDENTS I VOTED FOR:

I REMEMBER WHAT I WAS DOING WHEN THIS TRAGIC EVENT HAPPENED (E.G. ASSASSINATION OF JFK, <u>CHALLENGER</u> SPACE SHUTTLE EXPLODING):

$\mathcal{T}$HE CLOTHES FASHIONS I WORE DURING THESE
ADULT YEARS:

*M*Y FIRST VERY OWN CAR WAS: ...AND THE
PRICE TAG WAS:

$\mathcal{S}$OME OF MY FAVORITE MOVIE OR TV STARS WERE:

$\mathcal{T}$HIS IS WHAT I WAS DOING WHEN THIS DRAMATIC ACHIEVEMENT OCCURRED (E.G. FIRST MOON WALK, POLIO VACCINE INVENTED, MARK SPITZ'S SEVEN OLYMPIC GOLD MEDALS):

$\mathcal{I}$ TRAVELED OUTSIDE MY LOCAL ENVIRONS TO
THESE PLACES AND REMEMBER THESE EXPERIENCES:

ONE OF THE NATIONAL NEWS EVENTS THAT MOST FASCINATED ME WAS:

*T*HIS EVENT RAISED MY UNDERSTANDING OF THE LARGER WORLD OUTSIDE MY IMMEDIATE SURROUNDINGS:

LATER YEARS

I WISH I HAD SEEN MORE OF THIS PERSON
DURING MY ELDER YEARS:

*T*HIS FRIEND BECAME LIKE A MEMBER OF MY
FAMILY IN MY LATER YEARS:

I DEPEND ON MY FAMILY IN THIS WAY:

*T*HESE DEATHS IN THE FAMILY AFFECTED ME STRONGLY:

$\mathcal{I}$ REMEMBER WHEN MY GRANDCHILDREN WERE BORN:

A GOOD TIME I REMEMBER HAVING WITH MY GRANDCHILDREN WAS:

$\mathcal{I}$ AM PROUD OF MY SIBLING(S) FOR THIS REASON:

M Y PREDICTIONS FOR EACH OF MY GRANDCHILDREN ARE THESE:

OF ALL MY PERSONALITY TRAITS I HOPE MY FAMILY WILL REMEMBER THIS ONE ABOUT ME:

$\mathcal{I}$ THINK I HAVE THIS TRAIT MORE NOW THAN IN MY EARLIER YEARS:

_I_F I HAVE A FAVORITE PERIOD OF MY LIFE IT WAS THIS:

THE BEST PART ABOUT MARRIAGE IS:

THE HARDEST PART ABOUT MARRIAGE IS:

A GOOD FAMILY IS ONE THAT:

I LEARNED THAT LIVING A FULFILLED LIFE
INCLUDES THESE IMPORTANT THINGS:

THE STRENGTHS AND CHARACTERISTICS OF EACH OF MY CHILDREN ARE:

As I approach the end of my life my attitude towards death is:

I WAS SAD WHEN I HEARD THIS DEAR FRIEND DIED:

THIS PERSON HAS STAYED WITH ME THROUGH THICK AND THIN OVER THE YEARS:

New friends I have made include:

$\mathcal{T}$HINGS I LOOK FOR IN A FRIEND NOW ARE:

What I like to do most with friends is:

A FUNNY THING THAT HAPPENED TO ME AND A FRIEND WAS:

A FRIEND TOLD ME THESE GOOD JOKES:

I STAYED BY THESE FRIENDS WHEN THEY WERE
GOING THROUGH A DIFFICULT EMOTIONAL PERIOD:

$\mathcal{T}$HIS GOOD FRIEND TAUGHT ME THIS IMPORTANT LESSON ABOUT LIFE:

I AM NEVER TOO OLD TO LEARN SOMETHING NEW. THE MOST RECENT NEW THING I LEARNED WAS:

_**A**_FTER I RETIRED I TOOK TRAINING CLASSES IN
THE FOLLOWING AREAS:

THIS TRAVEL PERIOD WAS ENLIGHTENING FOR ME:

MY FAVORITE PLACE WAS:

_M_Y CURRENT RELATIONSHIP TO THE CHURCH IS THIS:

OF ALL THE CULTURAL ARTS I LOVE THIS THE BEST:

I LEARNED A LOT FROM THIS VOLUNTEER ORGANIZATION:

$\mathcal{S}$OME GAMES ARE ALSO EDUCATIONAL. THIS IS ONE OF MY FAVORITES:

*E*VEN AFTER I "OFFICIALLY" RETIRED I STILL DID THIS KIND OF WORK:

SOME RESPONSIBILITIES NEVER END:

THIS IS WHAT I THINK ABOUT "MONEY MANAGEMENT":

HERE IS A HABIT I PICKED UP DURING MY WORKING YEARS AND CARRIED OVER INTO MY RETIREMENT YEARS:

*M*Y BRUSHES WITH FAME WERE:

SOME OF MY FAVORITE MEALS/RECIPES INCLUDE:

I HAVE ALWAYS BEEN INTERESTED IN THIS HOBBY:

I HAVE RECENTLY PICKED UP AN INTEREST IN
THIS HOBBY:

I RETIRED IN THIS PLACE WITH THESE PEOPLE:

*I*F MY VISION HAD BEEN 20/20 THROUGHOUT MY LIFE I WOULD HAVE DONE THIS DIFFERENTLY:

THIS IS AN ACCOMPLISHMENT I HAVE ACHIEVED:

_T_HIS PRESIDENT HAS DONE A GREAT JOB FOR
AMERICA:

My VIEWS ABOUT SOME THINGS HAVE CHANGED OVER THE YEARS:

My HOPE FOR THE NATION IS THAT:

*M*Y HOPE FOR THE WORLD IS THAT:

$\mathcal{I}$ AM MORE/LESS TOLERANT OF THESE IDEAS AND LIFESTYLES THAN I WAS WHEN I WAS YOUNGER: